NAT
OUT OF
CONTROL?

*When God breaks
His silence*

NATURE
OUT OF
CONTROL?

When God breaks His silence

M. BASILEA SCHLINK

KANAAN PUBLICATIONS
Evangelical Sisterhood of Mary
Darmstadt, Germany and Radlett, England

Copyright © 1994 Evangelical Sisterhood of Mary

Original title: *Wenn Gott aus Seinem Schweigen tritt*

First German edition 1994

German manuscript completed by early March 1994.
Translated from the German.

First British edition 1994
published by Kanaan Publications

ISBN 1 897647 07 7

Designed and Produced in England by
Nuprint Ltd, Station Road, Harpenden, Herts AL5 4SE

Contents

When God Breaks His Silence

Over thirty years ago the dedication of the Herald Chapel at Kanaan* was celebrated with a play written especially for the occasion. In *Lo, He Comes* scenes of end-time Christians facing the temptations of moral laxity, materialism, compromise and deception, alternate with scenes of angels worshipping God. As the drama unfolds, the sound of lamenting can be heard. The angel choir pleads with mankind and grieves with God, because the winepress is full to overflowing with the wickedness of humanity (Joel 3:13).

---

* Located near Darmstadt, Germany, 'Kanaan' is the headquarters of the Evangelical Sisterhood of Mary, an international, interdenominational organization, founded in 1947 within the framework of the German Evangelical (Protestant) Church.

Lord, how long will You wait
until You establish Your rule?
Has the moment not yet come?
O Lord, how humble You are!
You empty Yourself of Your power,
allowing people to mock and despise You
as once long ago when You walked the earth...

Yes, Lord and God, Ruler of all,
just and true are Your judgments,
for You are loving and patient.

You do not want anyone to perish
but want all to come to repentance.
How patient You are, O loving God and Father!

Come forward, O everlasting, omnipotent God,
and show what You are like.
To the godless You are a Judge
but to the contrite of heart
You are merciful and gracious.

Today, before our very eyes, the eternal God is
showing what He is like. Once again He is break-
ing His silence and taking action, as the whole
world is witnessing. In the summer of 1993 it was as
if the floodgates of the sky were opened. In America nearly 17,000 square miles of lowlands along the
Mississippi and Missouri Rivers—an area the size
of Switzerland—were inundated. The press wrote
of a Great Flood caused by a totally abnormal

series of thunderstorms.[1] Abnormal is the word. The cataclysm was impossible to predict. Since this flood of the century various parts of the world have been stricken with disaster almost unremittingly. Some examples follow:

- Severe flooding, landslides and mudslides in India, Nepal and Bangladesh, leaving about seven million homeless.

- Violent storms, flooding and several earthquakes in Japan, including an exceptionally lengthy tremor in the northwest sending vibrations as far as Russia and Korea.

- In Africa and on the Arabian Peninsula huge swarms of locusts destroying all vegetation. In central Europe a massive invasion of gypsy moth caterpillars defoliating extensive wooded regions and turning them into a winter landscape in summer. In Venezuela a butterfly plague causing rashes and fever.

- Repeated scenes of devastation after tornadoes and hurricanes in Central America and the United States.

- Extensive forest fires in Italy, Spain and France.

- Major earthquake leaving over 21,000 dead in a region of India previously little prone to earthquakes.

- In the late summer of 1993 torrential rainfall with catastrophic flooding in southern Switzerland, especially Valais and Ticino, as well as north Italy and south France. At Christmas and again at the turn of the year flooding disasters in Germany, Holland and France.

- Disastrous, at times uncontrollable, fires in late October and early November 1993 in California, and then in January 1994 in Australia, penetrating even residential areas and causing untold damage.

- Record sub-zero temperatures with masses of snow in America's Mid-West and East, bringing life to a standstill in many states as well as Washington D.C.

- The severe earthquake on 17 January 1994 in the Los Angeles area, with thousands of aftershocks, described as one of the most traumatic natural disasters in the history of the United States.[2]

So noticeable is this spate of disasters that even non-believers can sense that there is no natural explanation. Many find the unleashing of the forces of nature ominous. Fear sets in. Others say, 'Oh, there have always been natural disasters...' But there is no denying the fact that they have dramatically increased in recent times. This is intervention from on high. God Himself is taking action. For sheer force, frequency and simultaneity the catastrophes happening worldwide are unprecedented. We are experiencing the greatness and omnipotence of God.

A Swiss insurance company which for over twenty years has monitored damages resulting from all major catastrophes around the world concluded: 'During the last five years natural calamities have become increasingly destructive, in drastic contrast to previous years.' For the sudden rise in damages the experts have only one explanation: the markedly growing frequency and intensity of natural disasters.[3]

With one calamity following the other, people are gripped with a sense of fear and desperation. Residents in the California earthquake zone lived in a state of shock for days. Tens of thousands of homeless victims camped in the open or lived in hastily erected tent cities. Many slept in their clothes, always on the alert for the next quake. In the Los Angeles area over 3000 aftershocks were registered till late January, some being considerable tremors in their own right.[4]

While the earth shook in California, arctic cold hit extensive parts of the United States with abnormally low temperatures. In many states traffic was paralysed, and all business shut down. Air terminals, government offices and schools closed. There were widespread power failures. At the time of writing the media continues to bring news of disasters ranging from blizzards with record snow-fall in the East to landslides and mudslides in California, where the hillsides scorched by the wildfires of autumn 1993 were unable to retain the soil. Many residences, already damaged by fire, sank in mud.

During the Australian bushfires, as the inferno headed for Sydney, a columnist reported, 'In sub-urban streets no one slept. They watched the ugly rim of fire coming closer.' Perhaps the most start-ling aspect of the fires was the speed with which they attacked. Fireballs vaulted over houses. They would leave one untouched, then descend on another, consuming it completely. Fleeing residents often had no time to pack essentials or even put on shoes, escaping literally only with their lives. Many Australians recounted that during those brief hours images were etched on their memories that will never be erased, scenes grimmer than anything previously witnessed. Some could not speak. Their stories were written instead in eyes that had seen too much.[5]

Fear has been widespread since God has broken His silence. Suddenly, in an instant, terror strikes. Some are taken unawares in bed, others in front of the television, still others in the swimming pool... And no one is able to halt the threatening calamity: earthquakes, tornadoes, fires, floods, extreme cold or prolonged heat, drought leaving parched soil and famine in its wake, plagues of locusts or ver-min, almost apocalyptic in their dimensions. The results each time are spiralling damages and often inestimable after-effects.

Commenting on Los Angeles, the press said, 'The future of America's second largest city as well as that of its citizens was forever altered.'[6] Nor is that all. The region has long been expecting a major quake, the 'Big One', which will have unimaginable consequences. Facing the situation squarely, the director of the Earthquake Centre observed, 'We've reached a point now where our models are predicting more Northridge-type earthquakes or bigger earthquakes in the future than we've had in the last 150 years.'[7]

Recently Canadian officials also warned of a serious earthquake of catastrophic proportions in British Columbia, specifically Vancouver Island. But no one knows when it will strike.[8]

In these days the eternal God is coming forward and demonstrating His power. Is there a connection between this divine revelation and the arrogant self-confidence of man, who thinks he can take charge and save the planet himself? Just two years ago, in June 1992, the UN-sponsored Earth Summit (the United Nations Conference on Environment and Development) convened in Rio de Janeiro, Brazil. Thousands, including world leaders, met in the awareness that many things on our planet had to be changed to ensure Earth's continued existence. At the opening session the noteworthy statement was made: 'We're either going to save the whole world or no one will be saved. I think we're at a real point of civilization change…"9

God is left out of the planning. Man has assigned himself the colossal task of saving the world from doom, presumptuously imagining he will soon have everything under control. He is convinced that he can prevent an age of famine, restrict the birth rate through family planning, and reduce the world population to a permitted size by means of abortion and euthanasia. He intends to distribute the wealth of the earth more fairly, do away with trouble-makers, redesign the world through drastic changes in the created order and usher in the golden age. He labours under the delusion that he has almost reached the goal.

Significantly, there have been changes in the world, though of a completely different kind. God Himself is at work. He is no longer silent; nor does He merely speak. He is taking action. The changes are mainly in the form of natural disasters, God's judgments upon the sins mounting up to heaven in our times.

These corrective judgments reveal that we are totally dependent upon what God does. Whatever His holy will sets into motion, man cannot prevent through word or deed. We are created beings and can do nothing when at God's command the earth shudders, tornadoes whip across the country, thunderstorms rage, rivers and lakes burst their banks, freezing cold or scorching heat prevail. As perhaps no other generation before, we are coming to know God through His actions. He is showing what He is like.

> He does great things which we cannot comprehend. For He says to the snow, Fall on the earth; likewise He speaks to the showers and to the downpour of His mighty rains. God seals up, stops, brings to a standstill by severe weather the hand of every man; and now under His seal their hands are forced to inactivity, that all men whom He has made may know His doings, His sovereign power and their subjection to it.
>
> Job 37:5-7 AB

It is painful yet awe-inspiring to experience God's sovereign acts.

A Sign of
Divine Wrath?

The prestigious *Los Angeles Times* asked at Protestant, Catholic, Jewish, and Muslim houses of worship, 'Is the quake a sign of God's wrath?'[10] The result: Most of the clergy interviewed 'absolve the Almighty of blame for natural disasters'. When man presumptuously 'absolves' God of 'blame' for the disasters, he absolves himself, maintaining he does not need chastening nor deserve punishment.

Yet God declares in His Word:

> Behold, I will bring evil upon this place and upon its inhabitants...Because they have forsaken me and have burned incense to other gods, that they might provoke me to anger with all the work of their hands, therefore my wrath will be kindled against this place, and it will not be quenched.   2 Kings 22:16-17

God does intervene through natural disasters, and it is our sinning that kindles His wrath:

> Make certain that you do not forget the Lord...Fear the Lord your God, worship only him...If you do worship other gods, the Lord's anger will come against you like fire and will destroy you completely, because the Lord your God, who is present with you, tolerates no rivals.   Deuteronomy 6:12-15 GNB

In Psalm 2 we read of what happens when the nations and their leaders rise up in rebellion against Him:

> How strange that men should try to outwit God! For a summit conference of the nations has been called to plot against the Lord and his Messiah, Christ the King. 'Come, let us break his chains,' they say, 'and free ourselves from all this slavery to God.'...In fierce fury he rebukes them and fills them with fear.   Psalm 2:1-5 LB

After Israel had sinned and fallen away from God, the prophet Isaiah interpreted the ensuing judgment:

> It is the Lord they sinned against, for they would not go where he sent them nor listen to his laws. That is why God poured out such fury and wrath on his people and destroyed them in bat-

tle. Yet, though set on fire and burned, they will not understand the reason why—that it is God, wanting them to repent.   Isaiah 42:24-25 LB

In similar terms he referred to God's judgment upon Assyria:

> See, the Lord comes from afar, aflame with wrath, surrounded by thick rising smoke. His lips are filled with fury; his words consume like fire. His wrath pours out like floods upon them all, to sweep them all away. He will sift out the proud nations and bridle them and lead them off to their doom.   Isaiah 30:27-28 LB

Centuries later, the apostle Paul wrote to the church at Rome as if he already had in mind many of the sins typical of our times:

> God's anger is revealed from heaven against all the sin and evil of the people whose evil ways prevent the truth from being known.
> Romans 1:18 GNB

If we take advantage of God's patience to persist in sin, we are warned:

> You have a hard and stubborn heart, and so you are making your own punishment even greater on the Day when God's anger and righteous judgments will be revealed.   Romans 2:5 GNB

Yet even here and now God is giving us a taste of His wrath when He breaks His silence. Are we surprised that the fury of the Almighty has been kindled against us?

In no other age has the eternal God been so shamefully mocked and viciously degraded as in the last few decades. Anyone insulting Allah or Mohammed invites the imposition of the Muslim death sentence and worldwide persecution, as has been the case with the authors Salman Rushdie and Rachid Mimouni. However, nothing happens to anyone vilifying God Almighty, attributing heinous sins to Him and using Him as an excuse for every imaginable vice. Instead, the most shocking blasphemies are justified as artistic freedom and even awarded prizes.

Our generation is sinning grievously against the living God. Even at church conventions and in supposedly Christian publications blasphemy and mockery of our Lord can be found. Yesterday He was theologically declared dead; today He is blamed for all the evils in the world. In theatrical productions God is ridiculed as a senile old man, a powerless figure who has lost his grip on the world. He is held up to scorn and called bloodthirsty: otherwise, He would not have let His own Son be crucified. By now millions have laughed at the portrayal of Jesus as Superstar, surrounded by scantily-clad female dancers. If He is taken seriously at all, His divinity is denied. God did not make the world, it is claimed; in classrooms and at

Sunday school children are taught that man is the product of random forces. Today many have chosen Satan, the opponent of God, as their idol. They acclaim him and trust him implicitly, even offering him human sacrifices...

In the face of all this, God was still silent. I will never forget a time in my life, back in the 1970's, when sin was beginning to sweep across our world like a tidal wave. I agonized over the question, Why doesn't God intervene, seeing that He is God and all power is His? Now a new era has commenced. The eternal God is taking action and we human beings can no longer ignore Him so easily.

Just a Coincidence?

Who can deny the connection between the horren-
dous natural disasters and the sins of our generation? In some places it is strikingly obvious. The
Blue Mountains, with a long tradition of witchcraft
and occultism, were among the main areas ravaged
by the Australian bushfires.

In these preliminary judgments we have a glimpse
of God's holiness:

> Who can stand before his indignation? Who can
> endure the heat of his anger? His wrath is poured
> out like fire, and the rocks are broken asunder by
> him ... With an overflowing flood he will make a
> full end of his adversaries, and will pursue his
> enemies into darkness.   Nahum 1:6-8

Pursue His enemies? Strong gusts of wind
whipped the wall of fire along an 800-kilometre

stretch of coastland, with flames rising to a height of seventy metres in the sky.[11] The blaze struck various suburbs of Sydney, which has gained a sad reputation internationally because of its annual Homosexual and Lesbian Mardi Gras Parade, an event shamelessly maligning God and His commandments. One year at this parade a God-fearing parliamentarian, who makes every effort to restore commitment to God's commandments, was vilified, as a huge papier-mâché caricature of his head was carried on a platter through the city streets.

Fire storms also rage almost every year in southern France, known for centuries as one of Europe's most occult regions.

Similarly, in California God's wrath did not descend randomly on an area. The epicentre of the recent earthquake lay in Northridge in the San Fernando Valley. After years of extensive research Californian geologists believed they knew all the faults in this area, and that they were in control of the situation. A vast system of underground sensors had been set up to give ample warning of a coming quake. But suddenly, without any forewarning, the temblor emanated from a previously undetected fault.[12] Nor was that all. For a whole week the media failed to mention that the earthquake had struck the hub of America's pornovideo industry!

In Northridge and two neighbouring communities, almost directly above the fault zone, nearly seventy companies produced more than ninety-five per cent of the roughly 1400 pornographic videos made every year in the United States. This entire industry was severely hit. Expensive equipment, cameras, masters and duplicating machines, as well as archives, customer files, and other business documents lay buried beneath the rubble.

'Quake rocks pornography industry' was the heading of an article which said, 'God's will or not, there is no doubt that the devastation in California's video-Sodom has been close to apocalyptic...With no exceptions—every company has suffered some major damage, much of it immobilizing.'[13] Other sources confirm that the studios and office buildings of virtually every major American producer and distributor of pornographic videos were damaged.[14]

Unimagined filth, deception, mental and emotional pollution have been churned out in this region and then offered to millions, especially to the young, as a poisoned chalice. Perhaps the 'Notorious Prostitute', Babylon the Great, mother of harlots, with her golden goblet full of obscenities (Revelation 17) maintained a stronghold there. To create these porno productions unbelievably vile sins and perverted sex, involving even children and infants, were practised. And all this while God has been silent.

But not any longer! In our days He has suddenly broken His silence.

A helicopter pilot flying over the area was staggered by the devastation he saw: collapsed

buildings, a flattened multi-level parking structure...
Shortly after the quake, a radio commentator
described a large Northridge shopping centre as a
ghost town. It was cordoned off by a chain link
fence, so that no one could enter. Sight-seeing
buses circled the place, with tourists on board taking pictures of the twisted rubble.[15] No one had
ever seen anything like it.

John's prophetic vision of the future in Revelation 14 and 18 invariably comes to mind. In the end
times an angel with great authority will descend
from heaven and announce with a powerful voice:

> She has fallen! Great Babylon has fallen!...The
> kings of the earth...will cry and weep over the
> city when they see the smoke from the flames
> that consume her. They stand a long way off,
> because they are afraid of sharing in her suffer-
> ing. They say, 'How terrible! How awful! This
> great and mighty city Babylon! In just one hour
> you have been punished!' The businessmen of
> the earth also cry and mourn for her, because no
> one buys their goods any longer.
>
> Revelation 18:2,9-11 GNB

Northridge may have been a foreshadowing of
what it will be like when the Lord begins to destroy
those who destroy the earth (Revelation 11:18). As
it says elsewhere in Scripture, 'At his wrath the
earth quakes' (Jeremiah 10:10); 'I will pour out my
wrath like water' (Hosea 5:10).

Will anyone dispute that God is behind such events? What person could release the forces of the earth with a single word and cause an earthquake or destroy whole areas through floods or tornadoes? Similarly, when the eastern half of the United States was afflicted several times by intense cold, was this not the Lord's doing?

> The storm winds come from the south, and the biting cold from the north. The breath of God freezes the waters, and turns them to solid ice. Lightning flashes from the clouds, as they move at God's will. They do all that God commands, everywhere throughout the world. God sends rain to water the earth; he may send it to punish men, or to show them his favour.
>
> Job 37:9-13 GNB

The same omnipotent God is now putting man in his place when he dares to exalt himself over his Maker. What human wisdom devises is reduced to nothing. Yet was not man discussing and proposing how to save 'Mother Earth'? For years now in various countries legislation to this effect has either been in preparation or already in force.

In America an Endangered Species Act is often radically interpreted and administered. The government alone decides the fate of areas where such species are found. Without consideration of property owners, the government can declare them to be habitats and impose land-use restrictions regarding agriculture or housing, for instance. There are cases of people being forced out of jobs and off the land for the sake of a specific kind of owl or tortoise. Water reservoirs, creeks and rivers have in some instances been banned from use, so as not to disturb certain subspecies of fish. Other examples could be listed.[16] In Germany, too, similar restrictions are being introduced.

One source states that under federal wetlands determinations, as much as 60 per cent of the total U.S. land area is 'wet'. As with the Endangered Species Act, this would enable the government to limit or prevent the use of land, without any obligation of compensation to the private owner.[17]

God, however, has let other 'wetlands' come into being. Not long ago countless numbers in various American states were brought face to face with the reality of the mighty, exalted and most holy God, in whose majestic presence man falls silent. During cloudbursts lasting for days they could sense the power of the Maker of heaven and earth, who alone can 'empty the cisterns of heaven' (Job 38:37 NEB). The waters of the Mississippi and Missouri rose and rose. Dikes broke despite immense efforts to stop the flooding. America's breadbasket was inundated. People were evacuated as houses, pastures, cattle and farmlands were submerged by flood water.

God is manifesting Himself in His awesomeness, which no man can fathom, as Scripture says:

Do you know the laws that govern the skies, and can you make them apply to the earth? Can you shout orders to the clouds and make them drench you with rain? And if you command the lightning to flash, will it come to you and say, 'At your service'?   Job 38:33-35 GNB

All this comes to pass through the action of the living God, of whom it is written:

When he spoke, the world was created; at his command everything appeared.

Psalm 33:9 GNB

What Next?

At the fall of Babylon, 'the businessmen of the earth' will 'cry and mourn for her, because no one buys their goods any longer' (Revelation 18:11 GNB). How seriously did today's businessmen take God's blow against the pornographic industry in Northridge? Soon after the earthquake, the manager of a firm selling videos, magazines and sexual devices commented, 'Religious fanatics might think this was God's way of telling us, "Hey, stop this filth!" '[18] A director working for several Northridge studios remarked: 'Can you imagine how (the fundamentalists) are going to leap on this when the smoke clears?...They'll say it's God's retribution, His personal destruction of America's most wicked city.'[19] In a television show a comedian mimicked God holding Los Angeles in the palm of His hand, shaking it violently and demanding, 'They're still making those porno films in L.A.?'—'God,' the comedian quipped, 'must be angry.'[20]

What does God have to send next to make us finally wake up? It was very much hoped that after the January inferno the city of Sydney would at least cancel the yearly Mardi Gras Parade, the homosexual carnival. But humanity seems to be determined to indulge in sinful pleasures to spite God.

Not only was the parade a lavish spectacle with 3500 active participants and over 130 floats, but it was even screened nationwide at prime time and advertised as a three-hour video. Massive protests against the telecast, including a petition signed by almost ninety Members of Federal Parliament and thousands of telephone calls to the Australian Broadcasting Corporation, were ignored.[21] Active homosexuals were reportedly employed to assist in the production of this TV special.

According to the press, crowds of 600,000 flocked to the inner city[22], in order to watch this shocking celebration of lust. Many had brought their children along. One float demanding the legalisation of homosexual marriages featured a gay wedding ceremony conducted by a 'priest'. Other homosexuals appeared in nuns' habits. A group of lesbians, dressed as brides, demonstrated for their right to a wedding day. Two Christian parliamentarians who make a public stand for God's commandments were ridiculed. The excessive display of near nudity and obscenity forbids further details. The television commentator, however, emphasized that the group marching that night included members of respectable professions.

This was just weeks after the bushfire disaster. Even while the fires raged, an Australian minister preached:[23]

> As we cry to God for mercy are we not acknow-ledging…that God is indeed in control of the situation—or at least that He can do something about it—and that at the moment at any rate He does not appear to be merciful but rather visiting us in judgment?…We are saying, 'Stop! We have had enough.' But when we say that, of course, then perhaps we have to be willing—as a Church—as a State—to hear God saying to us, 'STOP! I have had enough!'
>
> …When we have a Legislative Council, which legislates for immorality and against the revealed truth of the Bible…mocks the Word of God and seeks to silence the testimony of men and women of God…, then may we not be a people ripe for the judgments of Almighty God?

But the Lord is still waiting for our repentance:

> When I shut up the heavens so that there is no rain, or command the locust to devour the land, or send pestilence among my people, [or if I send fire, earthquake, flood, economic disaster…], if my people who are called by my name humble

themselves, and pray and seek my face, and turn from their wicked ways, then I will hear from heaven, and will forgive their sin and heal their land.   2 Chronicles 7:13-14

Does anyone listen to the voice of God? After the Northridge quake, a Californian minister wrote to the members of his church in the Los Angeles area:[24]

'Come, behold the works of the Lord, what desolations he hath made in the earth' (Psalm 46:8 AV). Such devastations are called 'acts of God'. They are due to His *permissive* will, designed to bring us to repentance and dependence upon Him. 'Who knoweth the power of thine anger? even according to thy fear, so is thy wrath' (Psalm 90:11 AV).

Many are capable of escaping reality through obsession with the sordid, while their fellow countrymen are severely afflicted by natural disasters. According to a survey, 60 per cent of the American public watched the Lorena Bobbitt trial, which was televised live at the time of the quake and the cold spell. The secular press concluded that everything else paled in comparison to a domestic scandal.[25] In this way people are distracted while the holy wrath of God descends.

Just how severely does God have to deal with us? Does He have to increase and intensify His

preliminary judgments? What a hardened generation we are! No sooner have the forces of nature
settled, the floods receded, the fires burned out,
than man impudently raises his head. He wants to
demonstrate that nothing can keep him down for
long. He will not allow anyone, including God, to
deny him 'the lust of the flesh and the lust of the
eyes and the pride of life' (1 John 2:16).

In all this we are beginning to see something of
the attitudes foretold in Revelation 9:20-21. Those
who do not perish during God's end-time judgments will still not turn from their sins in contrition. In spirit the apostle John sees that even those
directly affected by disaster will not repent but lash
out against the God who has power over these
plagues. They will curse His name and refuse to
give Him glory (Revelation 16:9).

Long ago the prophet Jeremiah lamented:

He struck you, but you paid no attention; he
crushed you, but you refused to learn. You were
stubborn and would not turn from your sins...

The Lord asked, 'Why should I forgive the
sins of my people? They have abandoned me and
have worshipped gods that are not real. I fed my
people until they were full, but they committed
adultery and spent their time with prostitutes.
They were like well-fed stallions wild with
desire, each lusting for his neighbour's wife.
Shouldn't I punish them for these things...?'

Jeremiah 5:3-9 GNB

A Move of the Spirit

When in January 1994 the bushfires raged in Aus--
tralia, shortly to be followed by the harrowing
news of the Californian earthquake, I was driven to
prayer almost day and night with such intensity
that it nearly consumed me. I knew that we needed
these corrective judgments of God. They were
inevitable. Yet my heart went out to the people in
the disaster areas. I prayed that they might experience aid, deliverance and protection as well as the
grace of repentance.

If only God's wrath would evoke contrition and
ignite a movement of repentance! That should be
our response. Only then can His judgments be
tempered with mercy. Time and again I sensed the
holy grief of God our Father. A cry welled up in
me: When the wrath of the Lord is kindled and He
has no alternative but to judge, we cannot ignore
His pain. Let us feel with Him and lovingly enter

into the suffering of those affected, humbling ourselves with them that God has to resort to such measures. Though we ourselves may be spared, let us not forget others but pray and plead for them all the more. During such afflictions God is appealing to every one of us, 'Repent, turn back to Me! I am waiting for you. I will make all things new.'

At every new blow of judgment heaven must be waiting for those afflicted to respond to the warning, 'Oh, wake up, wake up!—This judgment is from the Almighty, who may send something far more serious if you do not repent.'

The Lord is waiting for repentance and a radical change of attitude not only in the areas already stricken but especially among those who know Him. As believers we should so identify with the sufferers as though we ourselves were suffering and lead the way with prayer and repentance. In one way or another we have all contributed to the decline of our countries, the moral landslide, an 'overthrown Sinai', even if it was merely through apathy. By sending corrective judgments, God the Father seeks to draw back to His heart each one of us who has perhaps drifted away and become lukewarm. He is calling on us to humble ourselves before Him in repentance, to ask forgiveness and mend our ways, inspiring others to do the same.

We can only feel shame in view of our own sins and grieve with the Father, who is eternal Love. All who now weep that God is forced to use such disciplinary measures, all who love their land and nation, are called to repentance. The thought must grip us: God has broken His silence. His judgments are descending. Now the time has come for a widespread move back to God, so that His grace can be released as never before.

Will we make the most of this time?

Repentance is the call for today. Repent, for otherwise the wrath of God will continue its course through the nations.

O land, land, land, hear the voice of the Lord!
Listen to the message of His wrath, sons of men,
and repent while there is still time,
so that you will not be cast away,
and your land devastated
by His awesome judgments.

Well-known religious broadcaster Dr Pat Robertson, founder of CBN, addressed the people of America on *The 700 Club*, after a report on the Northridge earthquake and a brief survey on natural disasters during the last five years:[26]

With all the compassion in my heart to those who have been the victims, and the innocent victims oftentimes, of natural disasters, I want to say this about this country. We have murdered thirty million innocent unborn children in America, and we have said this is a constitutional right to do so. We have taken prayer and Bible reading out of the schools of America and have turned them into cesspools of violence and occultism. Adultery, which is proscribed by God, is rampant. Promiscuity is rampant. And now something that is called an abomination by God—homosexuality and lesbianism—is not only being permitted, it is being enshrined into law as a privileged class, and students in the colleges of America are being taught homosexuality as a sense of, they call it desensitization against their 'homophobic prejudices'.

...This nation has entered into a dangerous time where the accumulation of the last thirty years of rebellion against God is beginning to take a toll. Not only is the internal structure of our society falling apart in terms of crime, and drugs, and juvenile delinquency...But now God in His nature is no longer our friend but has turned in a sense to be our enemy, because we have offended a holy Almighty God.

Now God knows how to take care of His people in the midst of these troubles. God loves this nation. And why He is sending these things to us is as a warning. If we refuse to acknowledge what is happening, it is going to get more and more intense...

Folks, if we don't do something now, the wrath and judgment of God is certain on this land...But we can turn, we can turn to God, we can forsake our wicked ways, we can cry out to Him and we can say, 'God, heal and cleanse this land'...

So long as there is no repentance, so long as depravity continues unchecked in our countries, there will be no end to the natural disasters, which will actually increase in intensity. The *Associated Press* even dared to comment, 'It seems that southern California is cursed ground.'[27] A geophysicist with the U.S. Geological Survey in Pasadena, California, suggested that the region may be in for 'at least five more earthquakes as large as the Northridge earthquake', which registered 6.6 on the Richter scale. Another option was that 'we are building up the stress to a much larger earthquake' of magnitude 7.5 to 8. 'Only one magnitude 8 would be needed to release the energy of 30 magnitude 7 events.'[28]

God is not mocked. He will curb the forces of nature only when there are enough people turning from their evil ways and humbling themselves before Him. In God's sight these are righteous souls, because they admit that God is right to send judgment and they declare themselves guilty. A handful of them could make all the difference. For their sake God may still spare a place, as He once promised to Abraham:

> If I find at Sodom fifty righteous in the city, I will spare the whole place for their sake.
>
> Genesis 18:26

We cannot run away from God. When the winepress overflows with the wickedness of man (Joel

3:13), the day of His wrath will descend upon the whole earth. For the majority, there may then no longer be an opportunity to repent. Our response to God's preliminary judgments will affect our destiny at His final judgment.

It is not yet too late, for God is 'not willing that any should perish but that all should come to repentance' (2 Peter 3:9 RAV). As a matter of fact, here and there in the stricken areas a move of God's Spirit is becoming evident; rebellion and hardness were not the only reactions.

'The freezing, the floods, the fires. God's telling us something,' was the opinion of a man in San Fernando.—A woman in Pacoima commented, 'It's God trying to get us to reflect on what we've done, how we act. We are all sinners. It's a signal He's sending us.'—A Baptist minister whose church in Los Angeles sustained severe damage remarked, 'So many have turned away from God, so many have turned their backs on God. The Lord has sent us a natural disaster to bring us back together.'—In Sylmar a twenty-one-year-old student interviewed about the earthquake said, 'I was just humbled by the experience. It just puts into perspective who God is, how powerful He is and how little I am.'[29]

For an immigrant Korean couple who lost their home through the November '93 wildfires and their business in the January '94 quake, material possessions are no longer so important. 'I was not a serious Christian,' said the wife. 'But I hope that this will be a turning-point for all my family to lean on God more.'[30]

A high-ranking government official in California remarked, 'We don't call them disasters any more. We call them plagues'—a reference to God's judgments upon ancient Egypt.[31] In those days God punished Pharaoh for hardening his heart and the Egyptians for resisting God and not allowing the people of Israel to go (see Exodus 7–12).

In view of the devastating bushfires in Australia the Premier of New South Wales not only called upon people to pray but said a prayer publicly. Even non-believers took refuge in prayer. After the quake in California, many began to cry out to God. Where churches were destroyed, they met in gyms and tent cities. Thousands flocked to the services, giving thanks to God on their knees for what they had salvaged, and gathering strength to return to a daily routine shattered by the temblor, reported the secular press.[32] Friends related that in the entire region there was a real move towards God.

Today it is still possible to have an encounter with the God who is 'merciful and gracious to the contrite of heart', as the choir sang at the dedication of the Herald Chapel. The fact that God has broken His silence and is taking action means it must be high time to accept salvation before 'the Lord Jesus is revealed from heaven with his mighty angels in flaming fire, inflicting vengeance upon those who do not know God and upon those who do not obey the gospel of our Lord Jesus. They

shall suffer the punishment of eternal destruction'
(2 Thessalonians 1:7-9).

Lament for God's deep heartache,
Throughout the world lament,
That all whose hearts are open
His pain will comprehend.
Destruction is impending,
Judgment as never before.
Oh, call, oh, warn and rescue;
Listen to God your Lord.

Lament for God's great suffering,
Lament throughout the world.
Mankind is so corrupted
And brings God pain untold.
Lament, those whom He fashioned,
In His own image made,
Are horribly disfigured,
Their hearts by sin enslaved.

We mourn for God's great suffering,
Lament throughout the world.
We cannot cease lamenting
His agony untold.
No one can grasp how deeply
Mankind has sunk in sin,
Perverse and full of blasphemy,
Corrupt without, within.

Oh, weep and mourn, lamenting,
Entreat God without end,
That once again His judgment
And wrath may be restrained,
Because we beckon many
Home to His heart of love.
Oh, help to call and save them,
That He be not so grieved.[33]

Awesome in Majesty

Whenever the Lord stretches out His hand in judgment, people are overcome with fear and trepidation. Not just *one* nation but whole regions of the earth are being affected. His visitations seem unremitting. Many more examples could be added. The eternal God is a consuming fire (see Deuteronomy 4:24; Hebrews 12:29). When He increasingly demonstrates His power and sends great punishments, which none can escape, will our generation finally learn to fear the holy God as He deserves?

Suffering resulting from the preliminary judgments should teach us to fear not that which could cause our death, but rather the living God. He longs for our fear of natural disasters to be transformed into a fear of God, a reverence towards the Eternal One, who made us. Whether personally affected so far or not, we all need to stand in awe of the holy God. Then we will no longer be afraid of death, suffering and loss. Rather we will have a wholesome fear of God and His wrath and we will approach the Almighty with reverence.

Last year while I was away for some weeks, the Spirit of God spoke to me urgently, asking, 'Where is your reverence?' I sensed that for myself and our entire sisterhood this was God's foremost question in our times. The greatness of the immortal God struck me afresh. What are we before Him?—Sinful and insignificant. In the Mother House we spent several evenings together talking about a genuine fear of God. There was a new move of His Spirit among us, and we were deeply convicted of our lack of reverence for God.

We saw that the command to fear God runs right through the Old and New Testaments. There He is portrayed as holy, awe-inspiring and unchanging. Great and mighty is He! Man seeks to flee from the majesty of the omnipotent God, who rules the whole earth. He is the immortal God—He who is and who was and who always will be from eternity to eternity. All people must die, including world rulers and founders of other religions. God alone has power over death and life and the entire universe. He created all life, from the smallest flower to man, and the cosmos is the work of His hands. Reverently the psalmist describes the greatness of God:

The voice of the Lord is upon the waters; the God of glory thunders...The voice of the Lord is powerful, the voice of the Lord is full of majesty...The voice of the Lord flashes forth flames of fire...The voice of the Lord makes the oaks to whirl, and strips the forests bare; and in his temple all cry, 'Glory!'   Psalm 29:3-9

The heavens are filled with the praise of His glory. Ceaseless worship is offered at the throne of God:

Worthy art thou, our Lord and God, to receive glory and honour and power, for thou didst create all things, and by thy will they existed and were created...Amen! Blessing and glory and wisdom and thanksgiving and honour and power and might be to our God for ever and ever!
                    Revelation 4:11; 7:12

We human beings are as nothing before Him. In the words of Isaiah 40:15,

Behold, the nations are like a drop from a bucket, and are accounted as the dust on the scales.

We have God's testimony of Himself through His servant Moses:

I, and I alone, am God; no other god is real. I kill and I give life, I wound and I heal, and no one can oppose what I do.

Deuteronomy 32:39 GNB

And through the prophet Isaiah:

I am the only God. Besides me there is no other god; there never was and never will be. I alone am the Lord, the only one who can save you...I am God and always will be. No one can escape from my power; no one can change what I do.

Isaiah 43:10-13 GNB

Moses and all the people of Israel praise the Lord in song:

Who is like thee, O Lord, among the gods? Who is like thee, majestic in holiness, terrible in glorious deeds, doing wonders?   Exodus 15:11

And the psalmist confesses:

Who among the heavenly beings is like the Lord, a God feared in the council of the holy ones, great and terrible above all that are round about him? O Lord God of hosts, who is mighty as thou art, O Lord, with thy faithfulness round about thee? Thou dost rule the raging of the sea; when its waves rise, thou stillest them...The heavens are thine, the earth also is thine; the world and all that is in it, thou hast founded them. The north and the south, thou hast created them; Tabor and Hermon joyously praise thy name. Thou hast a mighty arm; strong is thy hand, high thy right hand. Righteousness and justice are the foundation of thy throne; steadfast love and faithfulness go before thee.

Psalm 89:6-14

Who is like the Lord our God, who has now broken His silence? None can compare with Him. The universe is subject to Him. The earth is merely His footstool (Isaiah 66:1). Should we not live in awe of this mighty God? By reverently bowing down before Him in His greatness, we will experience His grace. The fear of the Lord will be born in our hearts and we will lead our lives in the presence of God.

It is not sufficient to be well-versed in the Scriptures and to acknowledge intellectually that God is alive. With our entire being we should come to know Him. We need to have the right heart-attitude towards Him. Everything depends on whether we fear God, especially now in the end times when suffering will soon come to a climax. Our very existence hinges upon it for time and eternity, as is evident from Revelation 14:6-7:

Then I saw another angel flying in midheaven, with an eternal gospel to proclaim to those who dwell on earth, to every nation and tribe and tongue and people; and he said with a loud voice, 'Fear God and give him glory, for the hour of his judgment has come; and worship him who made heaven and earth, the sea and the fountains of water.'

This is God's message to our generation. We are to fear Him and give Him glory now before His final judgments descend. Only as God-fearing souls can we stand before God in the end times. As soon as we rebel against the suffering He brings into our lives, we open the door to Satan, the opponent of God. A rebel from the beginning, he tries to tempt us also to be rebellious, especially during God's preliminary judgments. This is why the apostle Paul writes:

Don't try the Lord's patience—they did, and died from snake bites. And don't murmur against God and his dealings with you, as some of them did, for that is why God sent his Angel to destroy them. All these things happened to them as examples—as object lessons to us—to warn us against doing the same things; they were written down so that we could read about them and learn from them in these last days as the world nears its end.   1 Corinthians 10:9-11 LB

We are to lead our lives in holy fear, the fear of the Lord, as it says in Philippians 2:12: 'Work out your own salvation with fear and trembling.' But usually we fear for our lives or the lives of loved ones. We are anxious about our possessions. We dread suffering, privation, any kind of loss. We would make every effort to save our lives, health and belongings. Yet Jesus says:

> Do not fear those who kill the body but cannot kill the soul; rather fear him who can destroy both soul and body in hell.   Matthew 10:28

We should pray with all our hearts for the fear of God. As Christians we have often lost sight of this altogether. The message of cheap grace has encouraged widespread self-complacency. Do we tremble at the thought that one day we will have to stand before the great and omnipotent God, who is our Judge and before whom all our sins are exposed? Perhaps we had even recognized and confessed them but then failed to turn from them. On Judgment Day they will testify against us.

The preliminary judgments are of special significance for Christians. They are meant to teach us to tremble before the holy God. Though called by His name, we often lack the fear of the Lord when it comes to our sins. Let us be honest. Who is afraid of being cast into hell? Not just the Old Testament but Jesus Himself warns us when He says, for instance:

Every tree that does not bear good fruit is cut down and thrown into the fire.   Matthew 7:19

If a man does not abide in me, he is cast forth as a branch and withers; and the branches are gathered, thrown into the fire and burned.

John 15:6

So it will be at the close of the age. The angels will come out and separate the evil from the righteous, and throw them into the furnace of fire; there men will weep and gnash their teeth.

Matthew 13:49-50

Then he will say to those at his left hand, 'Depart from me, you cursed, into the eternal fire prepared for the devil and his angels.'

Matthew 25:41

Not every one who says to me, 'Lord, Lord,' shall enter the kingdom of heaven, but he who does the will of my Father who is in heaven. On that day many will say to me, 'Lord, Lord, did we not prophesy in your name, and cast out demons in your name, and do many mighty works in your name?' And then will I declare to them, 'I never knew you; depart from me, you evildoers.'   Matthew 7:21-23

Jesus is not trying to make us afraid. Love is His motivation. He is warning us so that we will not come under judgment for time and eternity. God's preliminary judgments should be seen as warning signs, intended to alert us. They are meant to spur us on to accept Jesus wholeheartedly as our Saviour. They should be an incentive to battle in faith and claim His victory over our sins, so that His redemption can be seen in our lives. We need to live in the awareness of God's wrath and the reality of hell. Our eternal destiny depends on it.

'His mercies never come to an end'

It is true that in the natural disasters of our times God is revealing Himself in His holiness, His wrath over sin, His awesome majesty as Judge. But equally, if not more so, He is manifesting Himself in His love and compassion. In the words of the prophet Jeremiah:

> The steadfast love of the Lord never ceases, his mercies never come to an end; they are new every morning; great is thy faithfulness…The Lord is good to those who wait for him, to the soul that seeks him…Though he cause grief, he will have compassion according to the abundance of his steadfast love; for he does not willingly afflict or grieve the sons of men.
>
> Lamentations 3:22-33

Although the judgments God sends upon the

earth reflect His holy wrath, they are noticeably tempered with mercy. In the disaster areas many marvelled at the supernatural way people were protected or saved just moments from what would have been certain death. Their house may have been hit but their lives were spared. Or they were away from home or out of a particular room when the catastrophe struck.

According to eye-witness reports, the bushfires often stopped inexplicably right at the fences, back doors or windows of people's homes. Sometimes the trees next to the houses were ablaze, whereas the houses themselves were not touched.

After a long, futile battle against the fires, the Police Minister of New South Wales said that if in the next seventy-two hours they lost 'only' 2000 or 3000 houses, they would be doing very well, for they had given up fighting fires. They were concentrating now on saving lives and property.[34] In view of that official prognosis, it was miraculous that a mere 200 or so houses were actually destroyed.

An article entitled 'Miracle amid the storm' described a couple's experience in the badly hit Blue Mountains. They saw the firestorm suddenly tear over the ridge. In one-and-a-half minutes it reached their house, and they felt the searing heat outside the windows as it passed over. All around them was burnt, black and smoking, but somehow they and their house were safe.[35]

So even in the midst of divine judgment there

were many examples of divine mercy. Thousands in California, including the media, called it a miracle that not more lives were lost in a city of nine million. It was providential that the Los Angeles quake came on a public holiday at 4:31 in the morning, rather than on a normal working day during rush hour. Hardly anyone was on the highways when they collapsed. Moreover, schools, offices, stores and other large buildings usually teeming with people were empty.

In all this we can sense the love of God. His preliminary judgments are primarily warning signs. God is pleading with us, 'Turn around, come back, so that worse calamities do not befall you.' Will His actions and words evoke in us the right response? Will we now turn to Him with supplications, sorrow over sin, genuine repentance, humility and trust? If we did, we would experience ever anew the reality of God's promise to deal gently with those who fear Him:

Then those who feared the Lord spoke with one another; the Lord heeded and heard them, and a book of remembrance was written before him of those who feared the Lord and thought on his name. 'They shall be mine, says the Lord of hosts, my special possession on the day when I act, and I will spare them as a man spares his son who serves him.'   Malachi 3:16-17

He fulfils the desire of all who fear him, he also hears their cry, and saves them.   Psalm 145:19

This is why believers in particular have experienced many wonderful instances of deliverance and can tell of the Father's infinite love and mercy.

From our sisters in Australia we learnt that a young woman who regularly held Bible studies at home was in acute danger when a firestorm came suddenly. She and her husband lived in a narrow gully, which acted like a funnel, drawing the flames straight through with incredible speed and force as if in a wind tunnel. The noise was terrific—like a jumbo jet landing in the backyard. But when she cried to the Lord, she could sense His presence and felt very protected. It was like being in an ark, while the fire repeatedly circled around before it diverted from its path, leaving the house untouched.

A Christian family, who entrusted their home to the Lord before fleeing the flames, later found it unscathed. God had heard their prayers and the fire stopped six inches in front of the house!

A training centre of Teen Challenge, internationally known for its ministry to young drug-addicts, was also directly threatened. Two days after a bushfire broke out twenty-five kilometres away, the staff were not unduly concerned, for the fire had several large valleys and creeks to cross before it could reach them. That was in the morning. By 1:30 p.m. they were ordered to evacuate, and in the next twenty-four hours eight houses were razed in that area alone. Miraculously, their buildings were spared. None of the personnel and young people came to harm. However, their once beautiful valley is now charred and looks like a moonscape.[36]

A Christian radio station in California was wonderfully protected during the catastrophic fires of October 1993. On the first day 100 foot flames were coming straight towards the station. An emergency call to prayer was immediately issued to a large circle of friends. The fire struck so swiftly and the heat was so intense that a fire engine rushing to protect the station burnt up on the way. But it was as though angels were suddenly positioned around the station. The fire was unable even to touch one inch of the property, and the burning stopped five to ten feet on every side.[37] Beyond all doubt, we have a God who answers prayer.

A moving testimony reached us from the Californian earthquake zone: 'Early on January 17, I suddenly awoke with an eerie feeling. An unusual stillness alarmed me. Then, my...apartment began to jolt violently. The strength of the quake was so great that there was nothing I could do except to remain in my bed and pray. Despite facing the possibility of imminent death, I was very much at peace...Never will I forget the horrific feeling and sound of my apartment being wrenched into pieces...The first thing I noticed was that the place where my bed was located was the only untouched place in the apartment. I immediately gave thanks to God for sparing my life...What stands out most clearly is the great mercy and compassion of God, who is truly close to those who suffer...I know for certain that, come what may, God will not abandon me, and I can count on His continued love and care.'[38]

Others had similar stories of protection to tell. A young couple, violently thrown out of bed by the earthquake, grabbed the baby and ran outside barefoot with the crashing and rattling all around them. They praised God for their miraculous deliverance, because had they hesitated just a moment or two, a large wardrobe would have killed their child.

A minister friend of ours related that when the quake began, he immediately sprang out of bed to assist his severely disabled wife. The next moment a large television set fell on his pillow.

A family living only two blocks away from the epicentre were awakened by the shaking of their home. The husband held his wife and started singing a chorus based on Proverbs 3:5,

Trust in the Lord with all your heart
and do not lean on your own understanding.

When their daughter was able to leave her room after the initial shock waves, she joined her parents and sang the verse with them. They were totally at peace and did not come to harm. The girl narrowly escaped death, for a heavy dresser fell on her bed just after she had gone to her parents' room.

A letter from Northridge testified how God cares for the weakest and most vulnerable when the world around them collapses. Whereas the state university there suffered almost total devastation, with fifty-three out of fifty-eight buildings severely damaged, the department building for the physic-ally disabled remained intact. In this department 'there are two excellent Christian professors and some 250 disabled students attending classes...I do believe the Lord had pity on these specific people. You know, the parking building just next door is condemned. It is a miracle!'

In these days we see as never before that the greater our plight may be, the nearer God is, and the mightier His aid. Though the Father may place burdens on His weak and helpless children, He will always carry them with the load, sharing in their pain and distress.

Yet what a sweet aroma it must be for the Father's heart when His children offer thanks after tasting His 'tough love'! Nothing could take away their faith, not even the trauma of losing all their earthly goods in a natural disaster.

Moving testimonies were given at a packed-out Service of Thanksgiving and Prayer, in a com-munity severely hit by the Australian bushfires. A family man, whose house was totally wrecked, said: 'We prayed for a miracle and it happened. We were spared. We now have a strong sense of the

Lord's presence, so we know God is in control. We still have our main possessions—our lives and our children.'

A woman who lost her house and all her possessions came forward and read Exodus 3:1-17 from the only page left of her Bible. It contained the story of God speaking to Moses out of the burning bush and the promise: 'I will be with you.'

A minister, whose young family was made homeless when the fires destroyed the rectory along with the church, a school and ninety houses, testified: 'The church is people, not a building. We cannot see into the future but we know that Romans 8:28 is still the same today and "all things work together for good"!'[39]

Knowing the Father

In the end times when God manifests Himself in His holiness and awesomeness, not only do we have access to His grace as we bow down before Him in deep humility, but we may also approach Him as His children. We may say Father to the omnipotent Maker of heaven and earth! What could be more awe-inspiring than this?—God, the everlasting God, is love (1 John 4:8,16). Yet how can it be that the Lord God of hosts, who possesses all power and might, is love?

Love was God's motive for creating us. He really loves us human beings and always cares about us, although we are sinful and evil. He also loves all His other creatures and His glorious creation, the work of His hands. When in these godless times He has to stretch out His hand in judgment because of our sins, and whole areas are laid waste, He suffers far more than we. Only love can suffer like that.

Before heaven and hell God demonstrated how infinitely great this love is when He offered up His only begotten Son for us (John 3:16), so that in Christ Jesus we might all be sons of God through faith (Galatians 3:26). He loves us dearly as His children and for this reason He wants to save us. God's power and greatness go hand in hand with His love, which is His essential character.

When we humble ourselves before God our Father and draw near to Him, when we appeal to Him through our Lord Jesus Christ, we will experience His amazing love and faithfulness. We should approach the Father as loving, trusting children, yet always conscious of our sinfulness before a holy God. The one cannot be separated from the other, for in God holiness and mercy overlap. His glory, righteousness, majesty and greatness combine with His mercy, patience, faithfulness, goodness and fatherly love.

A genuine, wholesome and loving relationship to God is balanced between fear of God and awareness of our status as children of God, a balance which needs to be maintained. Both aspects are found in the New Testament. We are to be humble and fear the Most High, for 'it is a fearful thing to fall into the hands of the living God' (Hebrews 10:31). On the other hand, we are to love and honour our Father as His children, obey and trust Him implicitly, coming to Him with all our needs. As Scripture says, 'You did not receive the spirit of slavery to fall back into fear, but you have received the spirit of sonship' (Romans 8:15). Thus we may cry, 'Abba, dear Father!'

As we enter this relationship with God we will make the blessed discovery that our fear of God is transformed into a reverential fear, motivated by love. Then we shun and hate sin not out of a slavish fear of incurring God's wrath and punishment, but rather for fear of grieving God. Because we love Him dearly, we do not want to multiply His sufferings either by taking sin lightly or by being impenitent and self-righteous. A love-inspired fear of disappointing our beloved Lord and an ardent desire to please Him will now govern our lives. And this makes for joy.

Those who fear God and at the same time rejoice in being children of the heavenly Father do not rebel against God's leadings and chastenings. When tragedy enters their lives, they do not say, 'Is that supposed to be a God of love?' Such insinuations, as they well know, come from the evil one. Satan is particularly active when we are suffering. He tries to bring about our downfall through rebellion and despair. If we have really come to know God as the omnipotent Lord and loving Father, we will approach Him with the right heart-attitude:

Who is like God?
I am a mere nothing,
yet even so a child of Yours!

Then in every trial that comes our way, our one response will be:

> Father, it comes from You. And however You lead me is right, for You are love. I cannot tell what is good for me. Only You know that. And later it will become evident that in Your love You had planned the best way for me.

High as the sun and stars above
Are God the Father's plans of love
Beyond man's comprehension.
No human mind could ever conceive
The plans by which the Father leads
His chosen ones, His children.

Eternal, inconceivable
God's counsels for His children are!
How can I understand them?
God the Almighty's great designs
Never were made known to human minds.
Their depths are like the ocean.

My heart finds peace from all distress
When in Your loving will I rest
Like a small child so trusting.
My heart would yearn for nothing more
Than what You give Your child, O Lord.
Your will is best, my Father.

To You my life, my all, I bring,
For pain and loss are gain to me.
From Your hand I accept them.
Your will, so merciful and kind,
Measures exactly for Your child
What I can bear and suffer.[40]

Song in the Night

Living as we do in an age of suffering and affliction, we often find it hard to worship God. Pleading comes more naturally to us than praising. But it is to the believers in the end times that the angel in Revelation 14:6-7 proclaims, 'Fear God...and worship him who made heaven and earth, the sea and the fountains of water.' We cannot imagine how greatly the Father in heaven waits to hear songs of love, thanksgiving and worship from us. They would comfort Him, for He suffers the most when He has to demonstrate His wrath and send judgment.

He also longs to hear such expressions from us, knowing that we ourselves would benefit. As soon as we begin to worship the Father as eternal Love and praise Him for every token of His goodness in our lives, our sighing and complaining will stop. The darkness will suddenly be transformed into light. Singing a song of praise to God in spiritual night is extremely powerful, often moving the heart of God to intervene and do miracles. When Paul and Silas began to sing praises to God at midnight while they were in jail, there was an earthquake. The foundations of the prison shook, all the doors opened and the chains fell off the prisoners (Acts 16:25-26).

Praise and worship will transform our troubles. We will find that the Father is close to us and that He loves us. Our problems may not all be resolved immediately, but we will receive the strength to bear them. No longer will our burdens crush us. We will learn to see in them the Father's love and come to know Him at a deeper level. It will be a new revelation of Him, compelling us to love Him all the more as His children.

God is love and always will be. It is His name and His nature. Knowing this will bring us through every suffering, even martyrdom. How can His love pass us by and fail to help when we are distressed and hurting? It cannot, for

> His heart is love, His will is nothing but goodness and the paths along which He leads us are good.

Whenever my glance falls upon these words hanging on a wall in my room, I cannot help pausing for a moment to worship Him:

Your heart is indeed all-loving!
Your will, in whatever form it now comes to me,
is nothing but loving-kindness.
And the path You are leading me on is good,
even if I cannot understand it.
You conceived this leading for me
in Your loving fatherly heart.
It is good, whether I can sense it or not.

Peace floods our hearts as soon as we worship the Father in this spirit. When we are in the depths of distress, He gives us a measure of His joy, which no sorrow can take away from us. He is and remains the same—our loving Father, who cares for us in every plight and helps us. His love is unchanging.

What a glorious hope in the midst of suffering! Everything that touches our lives is part of God's loving purposes, for whatever we encounter or endure comes ultimately from Him who is eternal Love. His love is present in every cross and suffering He sends us. Let us therefore worship Him as our Father, who is never too late with His help:

Praise the Lord, who carries our burdens day after day; he is the God who saves us. Our God is a God who saves; he is the Lord, our Lord, who rescues us from death.

Psalm 68:19-20 GNB

Whenever the evil one tries to make me feel

discouraged, I oppose him with the triumphant declaration of faith which has been my motto for years now:

God is my helper.   Psalm 54:4

The number of times I have subsequently experienced God's help are past counting.

Even during chastening and affliction we can affirm,

All your waves and billows have gone over me, and floods of sorrow pour upon me like a thundering cataract. Yet day by day the Lord also pours out his steadfast love upon me, and through the night I sing his songs and pray to God who gives me life.   Psalm 42:7-8 LB

Or we learn to worship the Lord in humility like Job after all the calamities and personal tragedy he suffered:

Behold, I am of small account; what shall I answer thee? I lay my hand on my mouth...I know that thou canst do all things, and that no purpose of thine can be thwarted.... I despise myself, and repent in dust and ashes.

from Job 40 and 42

With this confession came the turning-point in Job's life, and his darkness became light.

What an opportunity we are given to overcome in our suffering! Have we ever found a dark and threatening situation completely transformed when in dire need we began to praise God as our Father? There is a phrase that keeps sounding in my heart:

The Lord our God does all things well.

At each new blow, each sad piece of news, each meaningless or incomprehensible leading, these words ring in me like the chiming of bells. Though God's dealings may hurt, He does all things well. It is right and best for me or for others. It is His perfect will. Everything springs forth from His loving heart, and His thoughts are always higher than our thoughts (Isaiah 55:9).

Even if the evil one is involved and seems to be directly responsible for the tragedy that has befallen us, let us remember that nothing can happen to us without the permission of our heavenly Father. Every event to touch our lives first comes under His careful scrutiny. So it will all serve to our good (Romans 8:28). Such leadings are often His way of bringing us to repentance. His ultimate purpose is to transform us and make us fit for heaven. One day we will see the benefit of particular sufferings. We should keep our eyes fixed on the final outcome: the heavenly glory.

The phrase that means so much to me is from a German hymn:

The Lord our God does all things well.
His will is always perfect.
To every leading I'll submit,
My spirit humbly yielded.
My God is He and in my need
He knows how to sustain me.
So I will trust Him wholly.

Samuel Rodigast 1649-1708

This hymn is said to be based on the song of Moses, which he sang when presenting the Levites with the law. It will be too late to learn this song in heaven. It has to be mastered here amid trials and temptations (see Revelation 14:3; 15:3). So it was with Moses, the servant of God, whose anthem of praise was born of the wilderness wanderings:

> Ascribe greatness to our God. He is the Rock, his work is perfect; for all his ways are justice, a God of truth and without injustice; righteous and upright is he.   Deuteronomy 32:3-4 RAV

In his Patmos vision the apostle John saw at the throne of God vast multitudes who had been through the fires of affliction. Their adoration sounded like the rushing of many waters, their praises like peals of thunder, as they worshipped God for His just and perfect ways. Worship is one of the special characteristics of the overcomers in heaven. It also distinguishes the end-time believers. Even now, while the preliminary judgments pass over the earth, the Spirit of God is awakening many worshippers who will one day join the throng before His throne.

Worship, praise, songs in the night. All this is to be born in us now during affliction. Nothing so glorifies God as praising Him for His love when we can no longer understand Him and are tempted to lose confidence in His love.

Loving Father, ever caring,
I will trust You without swerving,
Knowing You will help Your child.
You will keep my foot from stumbling,
Helping me stand firm in suffering,
Strengthened and sustained by grace.

Great, omnipotent Creator,
All of nature hails Your power.
For You, nothing is too hard.
You know how to solve my troubles,
Making paths in stormy waters,
Where I can in safety walk.

Faced with tragedy and trauma,
I will trust in You, O Father,
As the God of miracles:
Chastened daily, yet not dying,
Living on in spite of suffering.
Heaven's glory will be the end.

Father, I will keep on trusting,
Firm in faith and without doubting,
Help will never fail to come.
For what father under heaven
Would refuse his pleading children,
Give them stones instead of bread?

Loving Father, I can trust You,
Knowing You'll come to the rescue,
Helping me when in distress.
You'll not fail me or forsake me.
Though Your help seems slow in coming,
It will never be too late.

The Supreme Test

With the hour of trial coming soon upon the whole world (Revelation 3:10), how do we prepare? In what aspects will we be tested? Before an examination probably everyone wishes, 'If only I knew what specifically was going to be tested, then I would concentrate my energies on learning that.'

Shortly before the Passion of Christ began, He warned Peter and, by implication, all the disciples, 'Satan demanded to have you, that he might sift you like wheat' (Luke 22:31). Perhaps we, too, can sense that Satan is harassing and attempting to destroy us, bent on making us fail in the hour of testing to come. What will be at stake then? Jesus said to Peter, 'I have prayed for you that your faith may not fail' (Luke 22:32). So it will be primarily a test of our faith and trust. During the harrowing experiences of the end times the Father will ask each of us, 'Do you trust Me? Do you believe in My love when you can no longer understand Me?'

Let us not deceive ourselves. At the Last Supper, when Judas went out and the time of testing began for the disciples, it was night—not just any night but the night of which Jesus said, 'This is your hour, and the power of darkness' (Luke 22:53). In such impenetrable darkness visibility and communication are almost impossible. The God of love may seem totally incomprehensible in what He does or does not do, particularly in His silence when He conceals His power, withdraws the sense of His presence, and we feel abandoned to the mercy of Satan. Then the evil one will try to make us lose confidence in God and His love. If he succeeds, we will fail the test.

As the Book of Revelation repeatedly stresses, the believers in the end times above all need to have an unshakeable faith—implicit trust in God's love:

You did not abandon your faith in me.

Revelation 2:13 GNB

I know your works, your love and faith.

Revelation 2:19

Here is a call for the endurance and faith of the saints.   Revelation 13:10

Similarly, the Letter to the Hebrews urges us to maintain our confidence in the Lord (Hebrews 3:6) and not to throw away our trust, for it brings with it a great reward (Hebrews 10:35).

To trust God wholeheartedly, even when He seems to be against us, is possible only if we love Him. This is why the fear of God and a father-child relationship with our heavenly Father are vital if we are not to fail in the hour of trial. If we have come to know God as the great, omnipotent Maker and Ruler of the world as well as an ever-caring God of love, all the questions Satan prompts in us will dissolve into nothing: *Why does God permit such things? Why doesn't He hear me when I pray so much? Why doesn't He demonstrate His power? Why did that have to happen to me?*

If we have come to know God's loving heart and regard ourselves as nothing in the presence of the Eternal and Almighty, we will not lose confidence in Him. In every situation we will declare with implicit trust, 'I don't need to understand God. I am His child. And what child can possibly understand everything his father decides, says or does?' Indeed, how can we human beings comprehend the actions of the great, omnipotent, everlasting God, who is both our Maker and Father? What arrogance on our part to think we know what is best for us! Instead, let us become like little children, loved by their father and also loving him, utterly confident that he makes no mistakes. Let us learn to trust our heavenly Father, knowing beyond all doubt that He is love.

As His created beings and children we have no

right to oppose God and whatever His holy will may bring into our lives. Everything depends upon our unity with Him. And where does this unity come from? It springs from trust in God's love, which is always perfect and wonderful, even if His purposes may be hidden from us. What we can do is to yield our will ever anew to God and His holy will. This is not asking too much. By honouring Him as Love eternal and trusting Him implicitly when we cannot understand Him, we will prove our love for Him in the time of testing.

If we do not lose confidence in the love of God, we will be invincible to Satan. In the coming times it will become evident whether we really trust in God and can submit to His will. Whether we are victorious or whether we fail depends not on our own resources but on our love for God, which is at one with His will and trusts in His love.

Those who have been tried and tested like this in the refining fire will one day join the worshipping multitudes before the throne of God. If we could always understand God's actions, if we experienced nothing but miracles, we would never learn to be overcomers. What makes us strong is unity with the incomprehensible will of the Father. If we are one with the will of God, we are united with the all-powerful Maker of heaven and earth, the Lord God of hosts, who rules the universe. How then can we possibly be weak?

In an age when God has broken His silence and when His preliminary judgments are descending upon mankind, we still have a chance to go into spiritual training. Life in these end times gives us ample opportunity, as our faith and trust are tested in various ways. By saying Yes to the will of God and accepting His leadings day by day, we will be prepared for the coming hour of trial.

We will be richly blessed, for practising acceptance of God's will releases us from fear, depression and despair, even before the time of severe testing has begun. Instead of agonizing over His holy dealings with us or others, we learn to become trusting children of our heavenly Father, free from anxiety. Then we rest in the knowledge that even difficult leadings are good and beneficial, bringing us gain for time and eternity.

However, the growing frequency and magnitude of the preliminary judgments reminds us of the urgency of entering a genuine father-child relationship with our heavenly Father. We need to have imprinted on our hearts the very nature of God— the omnipotent God, who is also Love eternal and the Father of all (Ephesians 3:15). As His children we may grasp His hand as we approach the hour of trial. Then in every plight our one reaction will be:

My Father, I do not understand You,
but I trust in Your love.

If we keep saying this while Satan harasses us and the enemies of God persecute us, nothing can separate us from God. We will never lose confidence in Him and in His unfathomable will. Here lies the key to being victorious when the powers of darkness attack. By trusting in God's love precisely when He seems to be against us, we exalt and glorify Him more than ever. Before the seen and unseen world we demonstrate how highly we think of our Lord and God and how greatly we honour Him. Thus even in the darkest night we abide by the everlasting truth which is our testimony of the Almighty and Eternal:

God is love!

Notes

1. *Tages-Anzeiger*, Zurich, Switzerland, 23 July 1993.

2. Reuter, *Tages-Anzeiger*, Zurich, Switzerland, 25 January 1994; *Frankfurter Allgemeine Zeitung*, 22 February 1994.

3. *Topic: Informationen und Meinungen zum Zeitgeschehen aus biblischer Sicht*, No.11, November 1993, p 6.

4. *The Pat Murphy Show*, Radio KTAR, 28 January 1994, broadcast live from the Northridge area, and 31 January 1994.

5. Andrew Stevenson, 'The Fires of '94', *The Daily Telegraph Mirror*, 17 January 1994, p 13.

6. Nancy Gibbs and David van Biema, 'State of Shock', *Time*, Vol.143, No.5, 31 January 1994, p 14.

7. *Los Angeles Times* in 'More big earthquakes predicted for S. California', *The Arizona Republic*, 3 March 1994, p A10.

8. *London Observer Service* in 'Canada's "Big One" to surpass California's feared quake', *The Arizona Republic*, 29 January 1994, p A24.

9. *The McAlvany Intelligence Advisor*, Denver, Colorado, July 1992.

10. Larry B. Stammer, 'Is Quake a Sign of God's Wrath? Clergy Say No', *Los Angeles Times*, 24 January 1994, p A5.

11. Based on information from the Bushfire Control Centre, Sydney, Australia.

12. *Frankfurter Allgemeine Zeitung*, No.21, 26 January 1994, p N1.

13. William Arnold, *Seattle Post-Intelligencer*, in 'Quake rocks pornography industry', *Times Advocate*, 24 January 1994.

14. Jerry Adler, 'After the Quake', *Newsweek*, 31 January 1994, p 27.

15. Details from *The Pat Murphy Show*, Radio KTAR, broadcast live from the Northridge area, 28 January 1994.

16. *The McAlvany Intelligence Advisor*, Denver, Colorado, September 1992.

17. Ibid. See also Dr Dixy Lee Ray with Lou Guzzo, *Environmental Overkill: Whatever*

Happened to Common Sense?, pp 95–105, 230–232.

18. 'Das Erdbeben eine Strafe Gottes?', *Darmstädter Echo*, 29 January 1994, p 5.

19. William Arnold, *Seattle Post-Intelligencer*, in 'Quake rocks pornography industry', *Times Advocate*, 24 January 1994.

20. Larry B. Stammer, 'Is Quake a Sign of God's Wrath? Clergy Say No', *Los Angeles Times*, 24 January 1994, p A5.

21. John Stapleton, 'Flesh, feathers and fun as 500,000-strong party dances into town', *The Sydney Morning Herald*, 7 March 1994, p 5.

22. Heath Gilmore, '600,000 cheer parade', *The Sun Herald*, 6 March 1994, p 18; Deborah Bogle, 'Flesh, frocks and family fun make a Mardi Gras', *The Australian*, 7 March 1994, p 3.

23. The Rev Charles Abel, 'God's Judgment or God's Warning?', transcript of a sermon at St Paul's Presbyterian Church, Armidale, NSW, 9 January 1994, excerpts of which were quoted in February/March 1994 *CTA [CALL TO AUSTRALIA] Prayer Bulletin*, No.52.

24. Rev Dr Aaron L. Plueger of the Lutheran Church Missouri Synod and Interim Pastor of Ascension Lutheran Church at the time of the

quake, 'From the Pastor's Desk', No.II, Apple Valley, California, February 1994.

25. *Frankfurter Allgemeine Zeitung*, 24 January 1994; David A. Kaplan, *Newsweek*, 24 January 1994, pp 52–55.

26. Transcript of remarks by Dr Pat Robertson, CBN, on *The 700 Club*, Virginia Beach, Virginia, 18 January 1994.

27. *Associated Press*, as quoted by Dr Pat Robertson, CBN, *The 700 Club*, 18 January 1994.

28. *Los Angeles Times*, in 'More big earthquakes predicted for S. California', *The Arizona Republic*, 3 March 1994, p A10.

29. The last four examples are from *Los Angeles Times*, 24 January 1994, p A5.

30. Scott and Kim Lee, 'I hope that this will be like a turning-point', *Los Angeles Times*, 30 January 1994, p T10.

31. Nancy Gibbs and David van Biema, 'State of Shock', *Time*, Vol.143, No.5, 31 January 1994, p 12.

32. Michael Fleeman, *Associated Press*, in 'Victims' faith unshaken', *The Arizona Republic*, 24 January 1994, p 1.

33. See M. Basilea Schlink, *I Want to Console You:*

Songs of Love and Comfort for Our Lord in His Suffering Today, No.23.

34. Andrew Stevenson, 'The Fires of '94', *The Daily Telegraph Mirror*, 17 January 1994, p 13.

35. *The Sydney Morning Herald*, 10 January 1994, p 24.

36. *Teen Challenge News: News and Information from TC New South Wales*, Issue 1, January 1994.

37. High Adventure Ministries, Voice of Hope World Radio Network, December 1993 newsletter.

38. Anne McFadden, 'Surviving the Earthquake', *Catholic Twin Circle*, 13 February 1994.

39. The last three testimonies are taken from Ramon Williams' article 'Interdenominational Remembrance for Bushfire Victims', in *New Life: Australia's Weekly Christian Newspaper*, Vol.56, No.32, 3 February 1994, p 1.

40. See M. Basilea Schlink, *My Father, I Trust You: Songs of Trust and Dedication*, No.29.

If no sources are given, the stories are from friends.

Other literature by M. Basilea Schlink

REPENTANCE—THE JOY-FILLED LIFE
96 pages
'This book unfolds God's answer to one of the greatest needs in the churches of our time. If you are looking for new life, joy and power for your own spiritual life and for those around you, then this book is a must.'

YOURS IS THE VICTORY AND MAJESTY
96 pages
Readers comment: A stirring, dynamic piece of literature. ● The insight it gives about future events is something every Christian should know. ● How wonderfully the Spirit explains everything to God's children! ● The best analysis of the present situation I've come across. Profound, discerning. ● Superb orientation for our times.

STRONG IN THE TIME OF TESTING
96 pages
As Christians face growing pressures, the need to prepare for the testing of our faith is even more

urgent than when these texts and prayers were originally written. We would never be able to bear the hatred, harassment and persecution in our own strength. Yet, as Mother Basilea encouragingly shares, in Jesus Christ we can find all the grace we need to stand the test of suffering.

MORE PRECIOUS THAN GOLD   192 pages

A word of comfort, a challenge or a promise for every day of the year. As we explore the implications of God's commandments for our lives, we will be surprised to discover that they are not the burden they are often made to appear. In God's rules for living lies the key to His blessing upon our family, community and nation.

PATMOS—WHEN THE HEAVENS OPENED 128 pages

Vividly and arrestingly Mother Basilea takes us into the events of the mighty revelation once given on the island of Patmos. Today they are beginning to be fulfilled before our very eyes. This timely book helps us to see the age we are living in and will be a source of encouragement to us in these dark days. It gives our generation a completely new perspective to the future and creates in us a tremendous hope.

THE UNSEEN WORLD
OF ANGELS AND DEMONS   144 pages

We need to know our enemy if we are to defeat him. But we also need to know the weapons God has provided for us. After describing the origin of evil and providing evidence of demonic activity, the author focuses on the victory that is ours in Jesus Christ and the role of angels in the world today. For to assist us in the combat with the evil one, God has sent us the armies of heaven—His angels.